MISS MOLLY'S
SCHOOL OF KINDNESS

Zanna Davidson

Illustrated by Rosie Reeve

Pleased to meet you. Do come in.

Designed by Tabitha Blore
Edited by Anna Milbourne

Meet three little fox cubs,
Frankie, Felix and Freddie.
Don't they look sweet?

Only they're not sweet at all. They're very, very naughty. Worst of all… they are UNKIND. Here are some of the unkind things they had done so far today…

No! You can't have any of my cars. I WON'T share!

That's a stupid picture.

Where's my green car gone?

4

5

Their parents were EXHAUSTED.
"Maybe fresh air would help?" said Papa Fox.
"Let's take them for a walk."

The Fox family hadn't gone
far when they stumbled across
a rather unusual place...

"This way," said Miss Molly, showing the fox cubs inside. "Your parents will pick you up at the end of the day. But first, I think you need our help..."

9

"You're just in time for the first lesson of the day," said Miss Molly, taking the foxes into the THANK YOU ROOM. "Madame Merci-Beaucoup is going to teach you all about being grateful."

"Greetings," said Madame Merci-Beaucoup. "I'd like you all to start by thinking of a kind thing someone has done for you. Can anyone give me an example?"

It could be something your friend said, or something your parents do for you that makes you feel happy.

How to say "thank you" in different languages

Gracias

Terima kasih

Arigato

Danke

Asante

My dad taught me how to fly.

"That's a wonderful example, Billy Bat," said Madame Merci-Beaucoup. "Can anyone think of any more?"

The foxes hadn't said a word. "Don't be shy," said Madame Merci-Beaucoup. "I'm sure one of you can think of something?"

"I suppose," said Frankie, "even *my brothers* are kind to me sometimes."

"You see," said Madame Merci-Beaucoup, "kindness is all around us. Now, as you've all made excellent progress, it's time for your next lesson, in the BEING KIND CLASSROOM with Mr. Deer."

Mr. Deer smiled as they all came in. "We're going to begin by each doing one kind thing for someone else," he said.

13

But Felix had other ideas...

Sally got down from the table and burst into floods of tears.

"That wasn't very kind, Felix," said Mr. Deer, hurrying over. "Why did you say that?" "Because it's true," said Felix. "Skunks *are* smelly."

"Can you think of a way to make Sally feel better?" asked Mr. Deer.

While Mr. Deer was busy with Felix, Lily Lynx and her friends were building a tower. Frankie was feeling jealous...

Lily began walking towards Mr. Deer, holding
the tower proudly. Frankie couldn't help it.
She ran after Lily and flicked
the tower with her tail...

Over it went

with a CRASH

and a CLATTER!

Uh-oh!

Watch out,
everyone!

Yikes!

WOOMPH!

Oh, poor
Lily!

"That's definitely NOT being kind," Mr. Deer told Frankie.
Frankie looked at Lily's sad face and knew she'd done a bad thing.

I'm sorry, Lily. I can help you build the tower again?

Okay.

Frankie and Lily worked together to build an even taller tower. "And how does helping Lily make you feel, Frankie?" asked Mr. Deer.

HAPPY!

"Now," said Mr. Deer, when everyone had settled down again, "let's see if we can think even BIGGER."

"Even bigger?" said Felix. "What do you mean?"
"Kindness isn't just for friends and family," explained Mr. Deer.
"We can spread it around, even to those we've never met.
Can you draw your ideas onto this picture?"

Remember, even a small act of kindness can go a long way.

Give away clothes that don't fit us any more to those who don't have enough money to buy their own.

Hold the door open for someone behind you.

Make the street look nice for other people by picking up litter.

After lunch, it was time for the ADVANCED KINDNESS CLASS with Miss Molly.

"It's hardest to be kind when someone is unkind to you," said Miss Molly. "But it's good to think about WHY someone might be unkind. Let's take a look at the Map of Unkindness."

MOUNTAINS OF MEANNESS

Someone might be unkind if someone has just been mean to them.

VALLEY OF BLACK CLOUDS

Feeling blue

Having a bad day

Not feeling good about yourself

PATHS TO UNKINDESS

SADNESS STREET

Something sad happening at home might make someone not feel like being kind.

ALL ALONE ISLAND

Feeling alone or left out, or being laughed at, can make someone say unkind things.

Can you imagine going to one of the places on this map?

"How do you think visiting the places on the map might make you feel?" Miss Molly asked the class.

I know how it feels to be on All Alone Island.

I think I might be unkind if I lived on Sadness Street.

Will you play with me?

I don't want to play your silly game.

SADNESS STREET

Oh! I think I might have been to the Mountains of Meanness before...

Go away!

YOU go away!

I've never thought about WHY someone might be unkind before. It's really helpful.

"Next time someone is unkind to you," said Miss Molly, "stop and think a moment before you say anything back. Try to remember that someone is probably being unkind because of how *they* are feeling."

It's time for our next lesson now. Follow me everyone. We're going outside...

21

"You've all thought a lot today about being kind to others," said Miss Molly, "but did you know, it's important to be kind to yourself, too?"

I want you all to think about how you're feeling, and then work out how you can be kind to yourself. Remember, you can always ask for help.

I'm feeling bored. I need to find something to do.

You've come to just the right place. I have a long list of ideas...

Play a game
Read a book
Ride a bike!
Make a den!
Try hula-hooping
Count down from a hundred, while standing on your head...

BO BEAR'S SNACK SHOP

I'm hungry. Please can I have some food?

Yes! What would you like from my amazing snack shop?

I'm feeling worried about school. Can I talk to you about it?

Yes!

23

"It's time to think about the world around us," said Miss Molly. "It gives us everything we need – sunshine, food, water, shelter, even the air we breathe. How can we be kind back?"

25

"That was our last lesson of the day. Well done, everyone," said Miss Molly, handing each of them a badge to wear. "You've all done wonderfully at my School of Kindness."

Soon the grown-ups arrived at Miss Molly's to take everyone home.

It's time to go now, but remember, you're welcome here any time. And always try your best to be kind.

Thank you!

I've picked you some daisies!

I'm going to make you breakfast tomorrow.

Thank you for coming to pick us up.

Can we give our old toys to charity?

Papa Fox looked down at his kind fox cubs and smiled. He felt very proud of them.

"Wow," said Papa Fox, as they walked home. "It sounds as if you three learned a lot today."

We learned to be kind to others.

And kind to ourselves.

And kind to the planet!

Then Papa Fox tossed away his banana skin, humming a happy tune...

28

...the banana skin landed – SPLAT! – on a little beaver.
The fox cubs hurried to help him.

They all stared at Papa Fox.

"You didn't think about others when you threw away that banana skin, did you?" said Felix.

"Or the planet," added Freddie.
"Banana skins count as litter."

"Back to Miss Molly's School of Kindness," said Frankie.

"Sometimes grown-ups need kindness lessons too."

Hello, Papa Fox. Do you need my help?

Yes, he does!

The Fox family learned a lot from Miss Molly's School of Kindness.
And from that day on, the three little foxes were (almost) ALWAYS kind...

Design Manager: Nicola Butler

This edition first published in 2020 by Usborne Publishing Ltd.,
Usborne House, 83-85 Saffron Hill, London EC1N 8RT, England. usborne.com